AF598982

Safety During Activities

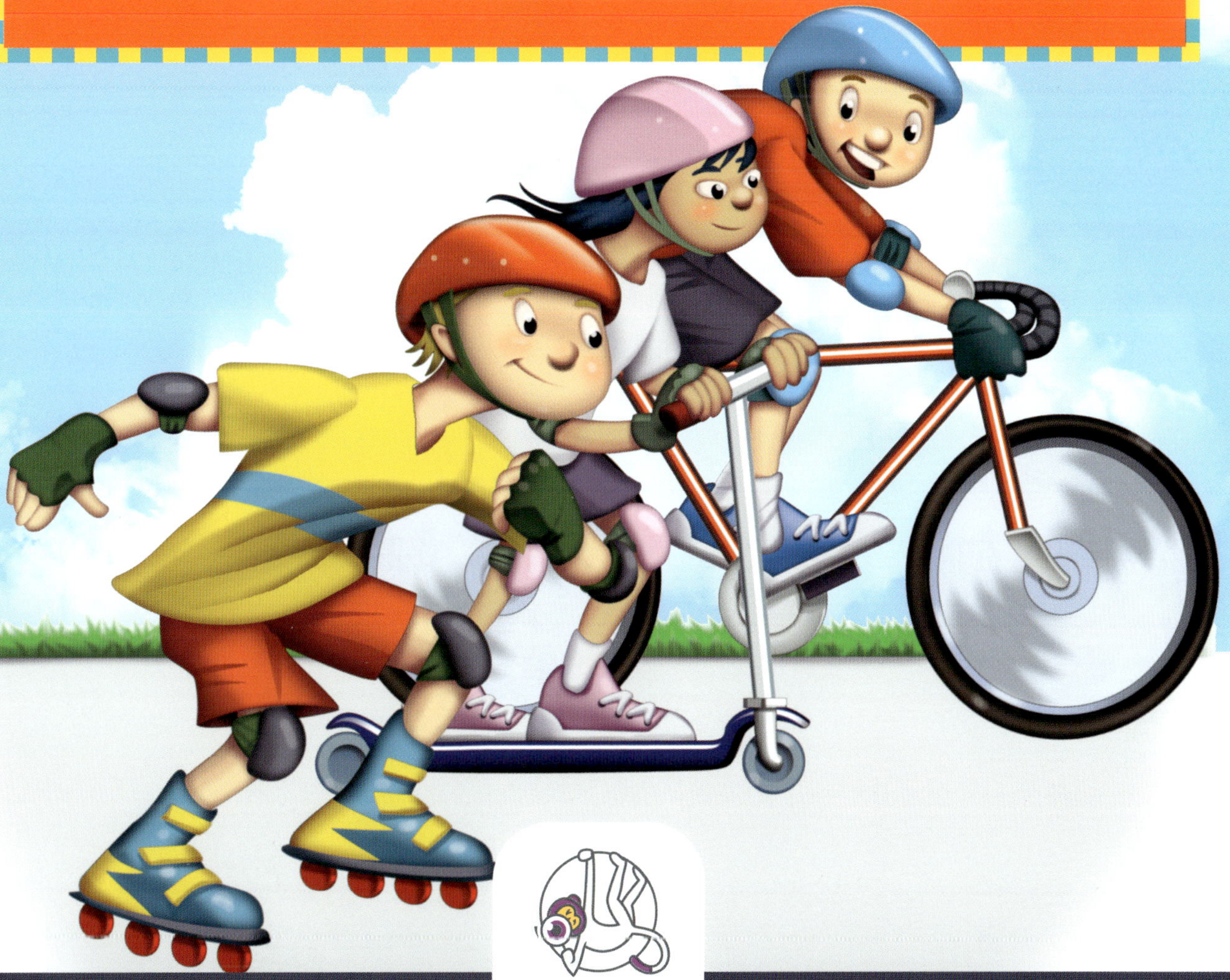

BY SUSAN KESSELRING

childsworld.com

ILLUSTRATED BY DAN McGEEHAN

Published by The Child's World®
800-599-READ • childsworld.com

Photo Credits
© ADragan/Shutterstock.com: 22 (helmet); Rubberball: 22 (biker); Photodisc: 22 (cone)

ISBN Information
9781503893986 (Reinforced Library Binding)
9781503895058 (Portable Document Format)
9781503895874 (Online Multi-user eBook)
9781503896697 (Electronic Publication)

LCCN
2024942729

Printed in the United States of America

ABOUT THE AUTHOR

Susan Kesselring loves children, books, nature, and her family. She teaches K-1 students in a progressive charter school down a little country lane in Castle Rock, Minnesota. She is the mother of five daughters and lives in Apple Valley, Minnesota with her husband and a crazy springer spaniel named Lois Lane.

ABOUT THE ILLUSTRATOR

Dan McGeehan spent his younger years as an actor, author, playwright, and editor. Now he spends his days drawing, and he is much happier.

TABLE OF CONTENTS

Safety During Activities

How do you like to ride? Is **in-line skating** your thing? Do you zoom down the street on your bike? Or do you like riding ramps and doing tricks on your skateboard?

Rolling on wheels is tons of fun. But you can get hurt if you're not careful. That's why you should learn how to be safe during your favorite activities!

Hi! I'm Buzz B. Safe. Watch for me! I'll show you how to be safe during activities.

Learning ways to stay safe during activities—especially ones on wheels—will help you have fun!

Having a bike that's the right size for you is important!

The Right Bike

Does your bike fit you? Make sure it does. A **salesperson** can help you pick a bike that is the right size for you.

Check out the bike's seat. It should be tall enough so your knees bend just slightly when the pedals are closest to the ground. Next, look at the handlebars. They should be as high as the seat. Lastly, sit on your bike. Make sure you can place your feet flat on the ground.

Safety Gear

Whatever wheels you ride, be sure to wear the right safety gear. Always wear a helmet. It can save your life if you fall hard.

Your helmet should fit **snug** on your head. The front of the helmet should sit about one inch above your eyebrows. Only one or two fingers should fit between the strap and your chin.

Some kids might think helmets look silly. But nothing's cooler than something that can save your life! In some states, it's the law to wear a helmet.

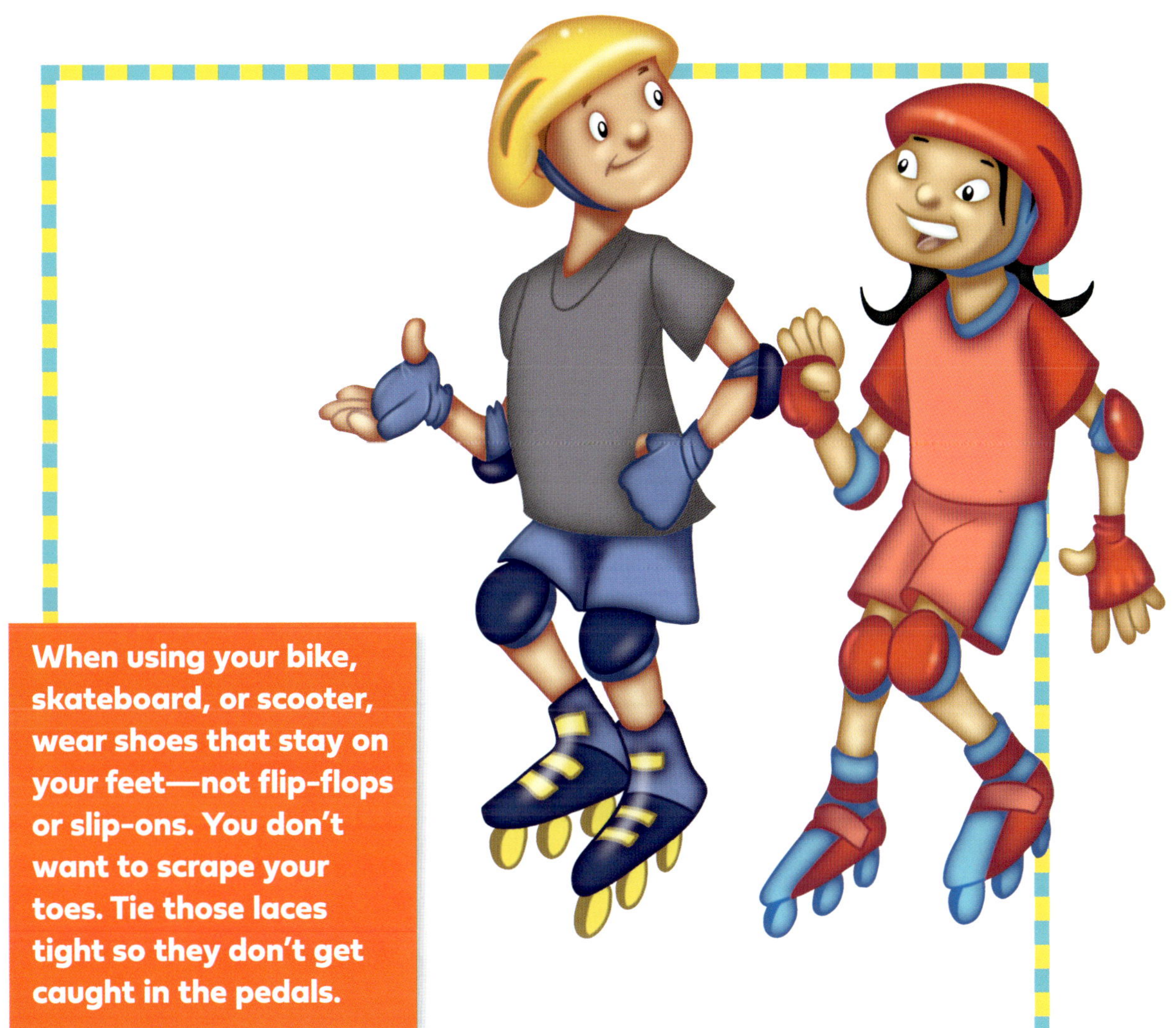

When using your bike, skateboard, or scooter, wear shoes that stay on your feet—not flip-flops or slip-ons. You don't want to scrape your toes. Tie those laces tight so they don't get caught in the pedals.

Next step—pads. On a scooter, wear elbow and knee pads. Add wrist guards for skateboarding and in-line skating. Pads can keep you from breaking bones and getting major cuts if you crash.

Safe Wheeling

Great! You've got your safety gear on. Now it's time to check a few things. Try the brakes on your bike or scooter to make sure they work. Feel the tires. They should be full of air. Check your wheels to make sure they're free of sticks, rocks, and other things. You're ready to roll!

Most wheels are built for one person to ride. Don't let friends ride your bike, skateboard, or scooter with you.

No matter what kind of wheels you ride, stay on pavement. Avoid dirt, gravel, and potholes. If you hit a bump, you could lose your **balance** and crash. Avoid wheeling through water. It could be slippery.

Putting your things in a backpack keeps your hands free to steer your bike.

Other Tips

On a bike and a scooter, it's always best to keep both hands on the handlebars at all times. You might have to quickly steer away from something. It's easier to do this with both hands on the handlebars.

Ride away from the road. Focus on the path in front of you as you ride. If you need to carry anything, put it in a backpack or bike basket. That way your hands are able to steer the bike.

Keep your music off until after you're done wheeling. Headphones can keep you from hearing cars coming your way.

Safe Skateboarding

Riding a skateboard is cool, too! Be sure to ask an adult to watch. Try out a skate park. It is a great place to ride!

If you want to learn skateboarding tricks, ask if you can take a skateboarding class. If you can't, that's okay, too. You can learn a trick from another friend or an older sibling. Just make sure an adult is there. You shouldn't try tricks on your own.

The part of the skateboard the rider stands on is called the deck. It's made of wood, plastic, or aluminum. Most decks are about 9 inches (23 cm) wide and 32 inches (81 cm) long.

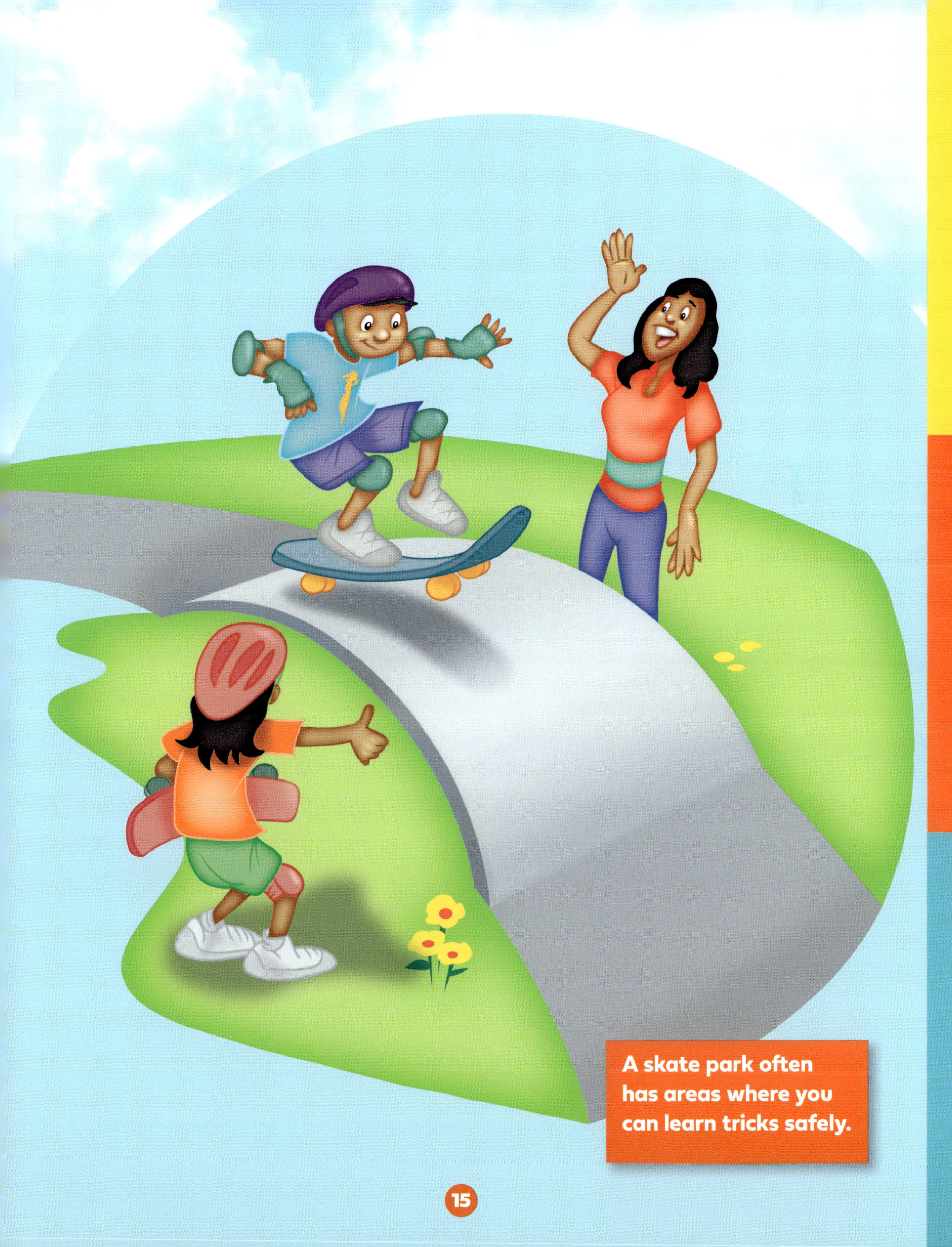

A skate park often has areas where you can learn tricks safely.

The street is not a safe place to ride. Stay on the sidewalk. Even better, see if an adult will take you to a bike path or a park.

Safe Skating

Have you been in-line skating? It is a great way to get around. But you need to know how to stop. Then you won't roll into the street or go so fast you lose control and fall.

In-line skates usually have brakes on the back. To use one, tip one foot up so the brake rubs on the ground. This will slow you down. Practice using the brake until you're good at stopping. Slow down when you go around a curve, too.

Always leave room between you and your friends when you're doing wheeled activities.

You can go so fast on wheels! Bike around the park, scoot on a bike path, or just skate down the block. However you're rolling, be safe and have fun!

Bikes with pedals were invented in the 1860s. Kick scooters have been around since the 1920s. In-line skates as we know them first appeared in the early 1980s.

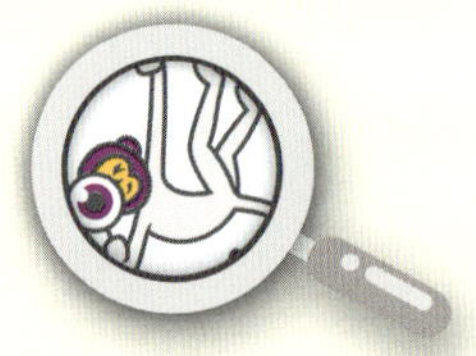

Activity Safety Rules

- Always wear a helmet.
- Wear the necessary pads and guards.
- Make sure your bike, scooter, or skates fit you.
- Check your wheels before you use them.
- Find a smooth, dry place to ride.
- Pay attention to what is around you when you are on your wheels.
- Have an adult nearby when learning tricks.

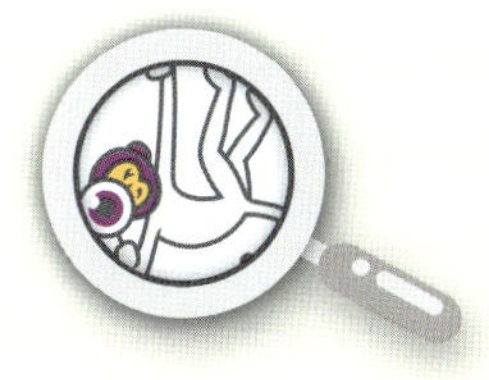

Wonder More

Wondering about New Information

How much did you know about safety during activities before you read this book? What new information did you learn? Write down three new facts that this book taught you. Was the new information surprising? Why or why not?

Wondering How It Matters

How does wearing the right safety gear make you feel when you're out doing activities? Do you feel more confident and safe? Explain your answer.

Wondering Why

Why is it important that your helmet fit properly? What could happen if it didn't?

Ways to Keep Wondering

After reading this book, what questions do you have about safety during activities? What can you do to learn more about it?

Safety Poster

Make a poster of safety tips to share with your friends for the next time you're all on your wheels!

You will need:

- Construction paper
- Markers, crayons, and colored pencils
- Magazines with pictures of bikes, safety gear, and road signs
- Scissors
- Glue stick
- Tape

Instructions:

Using your markers, draw safety tips on your poster. If you'd rather use pictures, use the scissors, tape, and glue stick to cut out pictures from the magazine that show safety tips. Now show your friends your Safety Poster before your next activity on wheels!

Glossary

balance (BAL-uhnss): Balance is your ability to stay steady and not fall to the ground. Ride your wheels on a clear path to keep your balance.

in-line skating (IN-lyn SKAY-ting): In-line skating is moving on skates that have all the wheels in a straight line. Always wear a helmet when in-line skating.

salesperson (SAYLZ-pur-sun): A salesperson is someone who sells you something. You may buy a bike from a salesperson.

snug (SNUG): If something is snug, it fits not too tightly and not too loosely. Make sure your helmet is snug on your head.

Find Out More

In the Library

Brown, Sky. *The Life-Changing Magic of Skateboarding: A Beginner's Guide with Olympic Medalist Sky Brown.* New York, NY: Magic Cat, 2024.

Jennings, Rosemary. *Safe on Your Bike.* New York, NY: PowerKids Press, 2017.

Kahn, Robert. *Bobby and Mandee's Bike Safety.* Sheridan, WY: Gotham Books, 2022.

On the Web

Visit our Web site for links about safety during activities:
childsworld.com/links

Note to Parents, Teachers, and Librarians: We routinely verify our Web links to make sure they are safe and active sites. So encourage your readers to check them out!

Index